I n the Middle Ages in Europe, monasteries were important buildings and communities. They helped safeguard learning and provided a sense of purpose to the people in hard times. Read on and learn about monasteries and what went on in them.

A Life Apart Together

Christians, in general, try to follow the teachings and example of Jesus Christ in one of two ways. The first way, which most people take, is to live a "normal" life—going to school, working at a job, being a part of a family—but to try to do all those things following the way of living that Jesus taught.

Why Were Monasteries Important in the Middle Ages?

Ancient History Books
Children's Ancient History

BABY PROFESSOR
EDUCATION KIDS

Speedy Publishing LLC

40 E. Main St. #1156

Newark, DE 19711

www.speedypublishing.com

Copyright 2017

Being a Christian is not just about going to church on Sunday, it means figuring out what a Christian would do in an argument at school or in a difficult moment at work.

There is a second way, which fewer Christians have taken and that is to withdraw from society as much as possible in order to pray, read the Bible and concentrate on thinking about God. At first people did this one by one, often retreating to caves in the desert in Egypt or the Middle East and we call these people "hermits".

Part of the attraction of this second way in the first couple of centuries after Christ's birth was that Christianity was illegal. You could be executed for following Christ and not taking part in the religious ceremonies related to Roman government and society. So some people preferred to get out of the way, even if it meant giving up all contact with their families and friends.

S ome hermits became famous as religious guides and people would go to visit and pray with them. The visitors would bring gifts of food or simple bits of clothing or perhaps ink and paper so the hermit could write down commentaries on books of the Bible.

S ome of those visitors stayed to live near the holy monks. St. Anthony, who lived in the desert in the third century AD, gathered a religious community around him without really meaning to. People listened to St. Anthony talk about the Bible and about God and tried to live as he lived.

St. Anthony

Religious Orders

As time wore on, there were more and more communities. Once Christianity became legal in the early 4th Century, living in poverty and contemplation was their way of offering their lives to Christ.

In the 5th and 6th Centuries, many religious communities grew both in the deserts and those closer to the cities. Some had very strange habits. It became clear there should be a better way of organizing the religious life that so many people seemed to want.

Saint Benedict

In 529 Saint Benedict created a "rule", or set of instructions, for living in a community of faith. These instructions detailed how the members of the community should work and eat, what they could own (very little) and how they should pray. Other "rules" developed over time, but all shared a basic set of principles: devotion to Christ and the church and a commitment to poverty, chastity (not marrying or having children) and obedience.

S ome orders gave up speaking as much as possible. Some developed beautiful chants which they sang together. Some closed their doors to anybody who was not committed to the group. Others went out into the world to spread the story of Christ, the "good news" or Gospel.

Monks

The men of these communities came to be called "monks", which comes from the Greek word for "solitary". In Latin, the language most of the Christian church used, a monk was "nonnus". When women's religious orders began, their member were called "nonne", the female form of "nonnus". In English, this became "nun".

Monasteries and Nunneries

As the monastic orders became established through Europe, they began to build places to live, work and worship. Often, wealthy families would give a monk's order land and money for building a church and a place for the monks to live. Having land meant that the monks had some independence and could grow their own food. Having their own buildings meant the order had a place to pray, to study and to teach. At one point there were over 400 monasteries just in England!

The monasteries were very important in reforming the Christian church. The church was the major organization still available when the Roman Empire collapsed in the 5th century. Many people at that time were more interested in power and possessions than in following Christ and they became leaders of the church. The monasteries helped to push for reforms that would end corruption and stop people using religious structures and property for their own benefit.

Monastic life

In general, a monastery was a walled complex of buildings. It might have many acres of fields and pastures beside the buildings, or not far away. From the outside, it would look a little like a fort and that makes sense. The purpose of the walls were to mark the difference between the everyday world and the world where the monks lived.

Inside the wall there would be a central courtyard, a space open to the sky and often with covered walkways around it. This was the "cloister", which comes from the Latin for "closed space." In the buildings around the cloister there were the church or chapel, places for the monks to sleep, an eating area and work spaces.

The monks needed a place to prepare wood and stone for repairing and extending buildings, places for making their simple clothing and places to study and do more careful work.

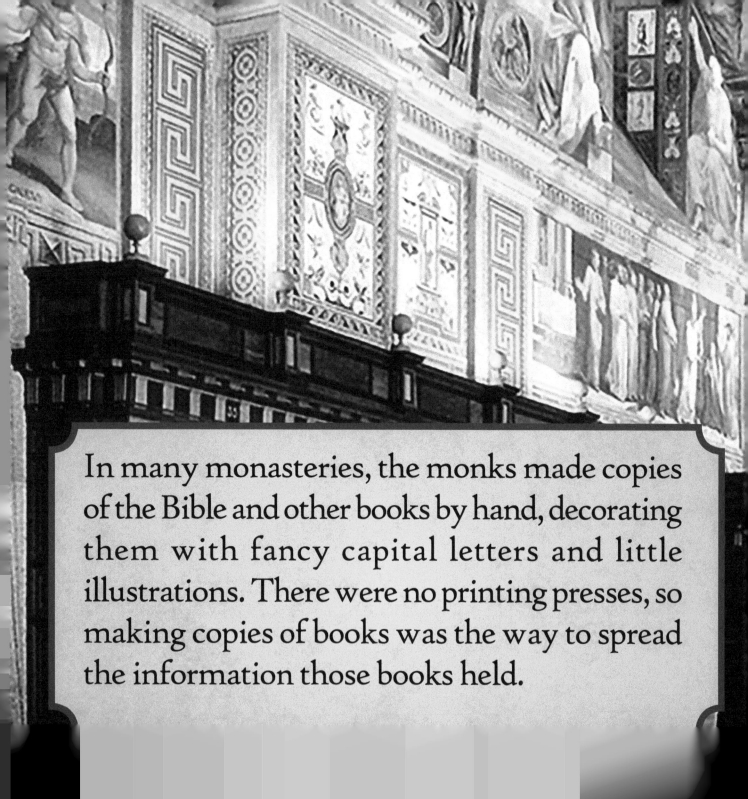

In many monasteries, the monks made copies of the Bible and other books by hand, decorating them with fancy capital letters and little illustrations. There were no printing presses, so making copies of books was the way to spread the information those books held.

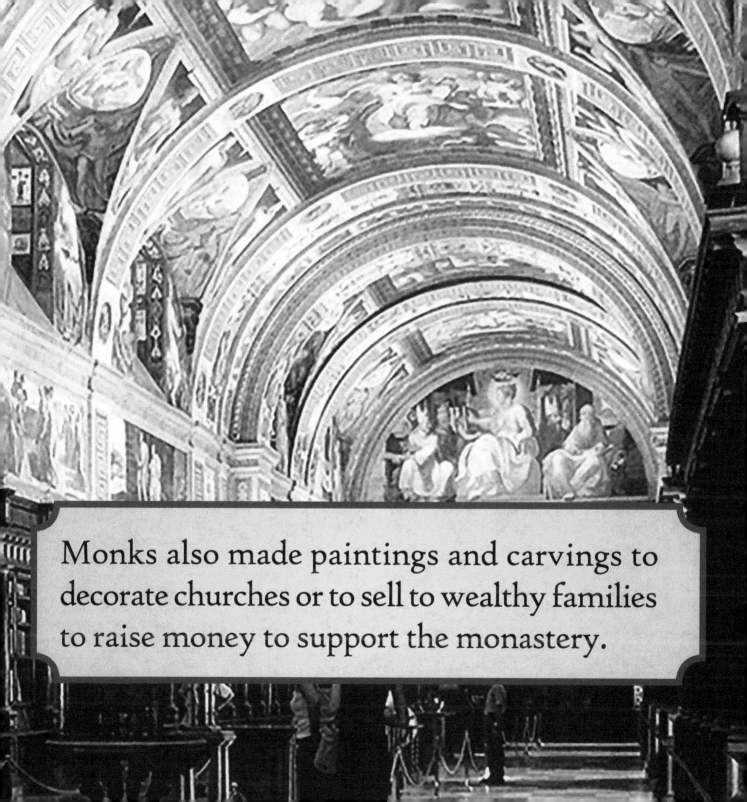

Monks also made paintings and carvings to decorate churches or to sell to wealthy families to raise money to support the monastery.

The main work of the monks in almost every monastery was prayer. There were eight times of prayer in the day, starting in the middle of the night. The monks would gather in their church or chapel to pray, sing praise to God and hear readings from the Bible.

In between services the monks would spend time studying the Bible, praying privately and doing physical work. Some would tend the crops and animals that kept the monastery fed. Others would work with sick or poor people in the nearby community, either going to them or taking care of them in a hospital within the monastery.

Some monks would serve as tutors to the children of wealthy families who wanted their children to learn to read and write. They would also help prepare people who wanted to become priests or monks.

The Importance of Monasteries

The monasteries played an important role in their communities. We will go over some of the parts they played in them.

Major landowner

The monastery lands would be extensive, and that meant the monastery often had food not just for themselves, but also to sell in the market and to give to the poor.

Refuge

In times of war or trouble, people often gathered in the cloister, behind the monastery's walls and gates, to keep safe. Pilgrims traveling across Europe would stay at monasteries rather than risking their lives in public lodgings or in a camp in the woods. At that time there were many as there were many lawless people who would set upon a single person or a small group and take whatever they had.

Charity

There was no system of hospitals, and very few doctors who were not connected to monasteries or the courts of the rich. The monks followed the instructions of Jesus. They sought to "clothe the naked, feed the hungry, comfort the afflicted and give shelter to the homeless".

Moral force

As nations developed in Europe after the fall of the Roman Empire, each country had its own king or ruler. That king often had the power to do whatever he wanted, and not all of them wanted to do good or useful things.

Often, the only control over a ruler doing things that would hurt many people, and perhaps lead his country into disaster, was the influence of the church and particularly the monasteries. The religious leaders had no armies, but they could point to the life and teachings of Jesus Christ, and encourage the leader to do better than he was doing.

PROTECTION OF KNOWLEDGE

The monks cared above all for the Bible, but they also collected and preserved books by many writers on many other subjects. The monasteries helped preserve wisdom and literature that would otherwise have been lost in the chaos following the collapse of the Roman Empire.

The Middle Ages are Interesting!

In the Middle Ages, people struggled against hard challenges to build their lives, feed their families and keep safe from their enemies.

The monks and nuns in monasteries and nunneries played a major part in making society better and helping people find a way to make a good life.

There's so much history to discover during the Middle Ages. Explore other Baby Professor books, like Why Were Castles Built? and Did All Knights Have Gallant Steeds? to learn more about the Middle Ages.

Visit

BABY PROFESSOR
EDUCATION KIDS

www.BabyProfessorBooks.com

to download Free Baby Professor eBooks
and view our catalog of new and exciting
Children's Books

CPSIA information can be obtained
at www.ICGtesting.com
Printed in the USA
LVHW050642170423
744483LV00008BA/634